Is your Bible discussion group all you want it to be?

Do you feel confident as a Bible discussion group leader?

Are you a skilled question asker in discussion groups?

Do you know how to handle someone in the group who talks too much or too little?

If you can't give a strong "yes" to all these questions, *Group Talk!* is for you!

Group Talk!

A Complete Plan for Leading Adult Bible Discussion Groups

Group Talk!

A Complete Plan for Leading Adult Bible Discussion Groups

ED STEWART/ NINA FISHWICK

Regal Books

A Division of GL Publications
Ventura, California, U S A

Other Adult Ministry Resources from Gospel Light:

How to Do Bible Learning Activities— Adult
by Ed Stewart and others

Creative Bible Learning for Adults
by Monroe Marlowe and Bobbie Reed

The Adult Teacher
Video Training Program

Adult Bible Study
Video Training Program

Rights for publishing this book in other languages are contracted by Gospel Literature International (GLINT) foundation. GLINT also provides technical help for the adaptation, translation, and publishing of Bible study resources and books in scores of languages worldwide. For further information, contact GLINT, Post Office Box 6688, Ventura, California 93006, U.S.A., or the publisher.

Library of Congress Cataloging in Publication Data
Main entry under title:

Grouptalk: a complete discussion plan for leading adult
    Bible studies.

   1. Bible—Study.   I. Fishwick, Nina.
BS600.2.G76   1986   220'.07'15   85-30142
ISBN 0-8307-1139-2

Contents

Part Four: Exploring the Variations

Growing into Group Talk! 115

Introduction:

Meanwhile, Back at the Bible Study

The center of the room was ringed with a collection of chairs of varied sizes and descriptions. About ten people were standing in three small clusters around the room's perimeter. One group by the window was admiring a newly cultivated window box. A recently arrived trio was greeting one another inside the door and a third cluster jockeyed for position around a friendly coffee pot on the table. The soft strains of instrumental hymn arrangements flowed from small speakers in the wall cabinet, adding to the warmth of the casual conversation.

A man named Roger invited everyone to bring their coffee cups and Bibles into the circle of chairs and be seated. After the introduction of a new member and a few more minutes of light banter about the weather and the success of the local high school basketball team in the state tournament, the group opened their Bibles and Nancy volunteered to read aloud a passage the group had gathered to study. The other members of the circle welcomed the words with their eyes and ears as Nancy read the short text slowly and confidently. At Nancy's invitation, Ollie softly invited God's presence and direction during their study.

Nick asked a question which launched the group into a discussion of the information in the text. Several in the group responded by identifying the main characters involved, a couple of stated commands and a promise attached to the faithful obedience to the commands discussed. Roger wondered aloud about the definition of one of the key words in the text and both Nancy and Valerie offered some helpful insights gained from previous personal studies.

Nick's next question provoked the group to expand on the meaning of the two commandments under discussion. Nearly everyone had something to say—a clarifying response, a personal illustration, an additional question which probed deeper into the explanation of the Bible study verses. Even Trevor, who rarely speaks in the group, surprised the members of the circle (and himself!) with a timely comment.

Once the discussion became so animated that members swerved onto another interesting but superfluous topic. Yet Nick's tactful questions and summaries gently steered the group back to the main track.

After nearly thirty minutes of lively, stimulating discussion on the meaning of the text, the group turned toward a conclusion with a question—again from Nick—which prodded each of the members to evaluate his or her own life in the light of the two specific commands they had discussed. It was quiet for awhile as individuals thought about Nick's penetrating query and framed their responses. Many remained silent and thoughtful as a few bravely voiced their need to comply with the directive God had issued through the soul-probing discussion. Nick spoke first, relating briefly how God had spoken to him during the week as he had prepared to lead the Bible study.

Vera took courage from Nick's example and asked the group to pray for her regarding a particular response she needed to make. Trevor was silent as usual, but nodded visibly, indicating his desire to be included in the prayer.

The chairs were simultaneously scooted into a tighter circle and the group members linked hands for supportive prayer. After a few minutes, during which several people interceded audibly for Vera, Trevor and others, Nancy led the group in a quiet, simple song of thanks to the Lord.

The chatter around the coffee pot seemed louder than ever as the Bible study group enjoyed their last steaming cups, offered and received warm good-bye's and headed for their homes.

☐ ☐ ☐ ☐ ☐

The preceding scenario is fictional, but it represents in concept literally hundreds of small Bible study groups across North America where people are getting into God's Word and, more importantly, God's Word is getting into people. From the days of the first-century church until the present, Christians have gained support and encouragement by doing what Nick, Nancy, Vera, Roger, Trevor, Ollie and others did in the opening vignette—gathering to read, discuss and apply the Bible to their lives.

Group Bible discussion is one of the most popular formats for Bible study today. The setting could be a Sunday School class, a midweek church group, a women's kaffee-klatsch, a men's Bible study circle or a home Bible study group. Successful Bible discussion groups seem to pop up in countless locations, in manifold sizes and descriptions, and at all hours of the day and night.

But successful Bible discussion groups like our opening illustration rarely "just happen." In addition to prevailing, bedrock prayer, several key elements must be employed to promote the kind of discussions which go beyond aimless Bible chatter or debate to productive levels of life-changing spiritual growth. Chief among all the elements which could be considered is the Bible discussion leader. Thoughtful, disciplined and prayerful leadership can make the difference between a boring, "doesn't anybody have something to say?" attempt at Bible discussion and an invigorating, growth-inducing exchange between eager Bible students.

If you are a discussion leader at some level of church or home Bible study ministry, we have some good news for you. For the most part, good Bible discussion leaders are made not born. No matter what your natural abilities may be (or not be!), you can develop the skills and disciplines which will help transform your Bible study group into a thriving, growing community. And the valuable tips outlined in the following pages are a perfect place to start.

All in favor of improving their skills as a Bible discussion leader turn to Part One!

Part One:

Reviewing the Basics

☐ What Is Discussion?

The dictionary defines discussion as "consideration of a question in open and usually informal debate" (*Webster's Ninth New Collegiate Dictionary.* Springfield, MS: Merriam-Webster, Inc., Publishers, 1984). But within the context of Bible study for adults, discussion has a narrower focus. For the purpose of this handbook we will define discussion as *informal group conversation which is centered on a Bible text and directed toward a meaningful goal.*

Let's look more closely at several of the key words in that definition in order to expand the meaning of discussion in teaching adults.

Informal. This term describes the atmosphere for effective discussion. It should be casual and nonthreatening. In the classroom *informal* suggests a circle of chairs rather than straight rows facing the leader. In home Bible study, informal discussion can take place in a comfortable living room or family room, or even around the dining room or kitchen table.

The informal quality of group discussion is also enhanced by the posture of the leader. The discussion leader should be seated with, rather than standing over, the participants. Sitting on the same level as the others in the group conveys that the leader is present as much to participate and learn as to lead or provide structure.

Furthermore, an atmosphere of informality seems to thrive where refreshments are available. A box of donuts, a platter of cookies or a bowl of fresh fruit within reach says, "Relax and help yourself!" And a cup of coffee or punch in hand often acts as a lubricant for the jaw, promoting cheery chatter which seems to open the door for serious discussion.

Group conversation. No, this doesn't mean that everyone in the group discussion talks at once, even though some discussions end up that way! Rather, *group conversation* means that everyone present is invited and encouraged to contribute their ideas throughout the course of the discussion. *Conversation* also connotes give and take dialog rather than a series of sermonettes delivered by each of the participants. Discussion group members should feel as comfortable about contributing to the Bible discussion as they would discussing the weather, gasoline prices, or their children in daily conversation.

The conversational nature of the setting again says something about the role of the leader. The discussion leader is present to encourage group conversation, not to monopolize on it. As such, the leader's skillful use of questions becomes at least as valuable to the discussion process as any comments he or she may add. The skill of framing discussion questions is covered thoroughly in Part Two of this handbook.

The word *conversation* also dictates the approximate size *group* which can be involved in successful discussion. The group must be small enough so that each member may take part within the time allowed. For example, you cannot have an effective discussion if you have 50 participants and only 45 minutes. Each participant will average less than one minute of sharing time, and even that will diminish if you have two or three "orators" who take more than their share of the time.

Discussion may run a little thin with a group of fewer than six and may become unwieldy with a group of more than ten. If you have a class or study group with 30 to 40 members, you need to break the large group into five to eight smaller groups for effective discussion. Six to ten is the ideal number for most discussions.

Some people see discussion as a series of simultaneous conversations taking place between the discussion leader and each member of the discussion group. However, a good discussion is one in which all the participants, including the leader, are freely interacting with each other. Each person should feel free to address a question or comment to any other member of the discussion group.

Centered on a Bible text. This handbook focuses on effective Bible discussions. As such, each discussion within this context must have Scripture as its foundation. It's true that the discussion techniques outlined in this book will be helpful in leading a topical discussion or a discussion based on sharing personal experiences. But the technique is most effective when applied to a specific Bible text which the leader desires the discussion group to explore.

The length of the Bible text under discussion will have an impact on the overall profitability of the group discussion. Basically, the longer the text, the more diffused will be the focus of the discussion; the shorter the text, the sharper will be the focus. It is often better to limit a discussion to a text of one to ten verses than to attempt a discussion of an entire chapter. The length of the Bible discussion period will be the ultimate factor in determining how much of the text can be adequately discussed.

Directed. This term says that a successful discussion must have a leader. In a small class the leader may be the teacher. In a large class, group leaders may be selected from among the learners and equipped for group discussion by the teacher or discussion leader. A discussion group without leadership is like a ship without a rudder. It may stay afloat—the group will probably talk about something—but you have no guarantee that it will reach its destination.

A ship's rudder is a good illustration of a group discussion leader for another reason. Though a rudder provides the needed direction for the ship, it does so in an inconspicuous manner. As the ship's steering mechanism, the rudder is relatively small and unseen beneath the surface of the water. Similarly, the Bible discussion leader can provide effective direction for the group without calling unnecessary attention to himself or herself. A timely question, comment or summary, offered from a non-authoritarian posture, can steer a group back onto course without appearing overbearing or manipulative.

The role of the leader in group discussion will be presented more completely later in this book.

Toward a meaningful goal. One of the dangers of using the discussion method is the temptation to use discussion for discussion's sake alone. We sometimes feel that a discussion is successful when all the participants contribute or when class goes overtime because people are so involved in the topic. But that's like saying, "These must be good oranges because there are so many of them." A Bible discussion is not necessarily a success just because everyone talks. The quality of the discussion is infinitely more valuable than the quantity of words.

Each Bible discussion must aim at contributing something specific to the process of Christian growth which is taking place in each participant. So the discussion leader must frame some specific goals for each group discussion in order to insure that the group actually arrives at a specific point of understanding and application rather than merely filling a period of time with conversation. Goals for discussion will be treated more thoroughly in the concluding pages of Part One.

☐ Why Is Discussion Valuable?

Next to the lecture method, discussion is the most widely used method for teaching adults. It's true that adults enjoy listening to a challenging speaker whose lofty rhetoric or down-home illustrations motivate them to action or renewed commitment. The lecture method does play a vital role in the teaching ministry to adults. But adults also love to discuss the Bible. And there are specific advantages to using the discussion method in teaching the Bible to adults. Perhaps an understanding of these advantages will prompt you to utilize the discussion method more often in your teaching ministry.

Discussion enhances retention of information. Several studies have contrasted retention in learning at various levels of learner involvement. When learners are only listening to a Bible speaker (on radio, tape, or non-illustrated sermon), they will retain only about 12 percent of what they hear. If the visual element is added (as with illustrations, diagrams, pictures, printed notes or outlines, etc.), learners retain approximately 50 percent of what they hear and see simultaneously. But when learners participate in the learning exercises—being actively involved instead of passively sitting and watching—they will retain up to 90 percent of what they say and do.

An effective Bible study discussion involves each participant in the learning process. By involvement in discussion learners will generally remember and apply to their lives much more than when Bible information is lectured to them.

Discussion encourages value formation. When individuals listen to a lecture, they are seldom called upon to respond to what they are hearing. As the lecturer states his or her case, the listeners (if they are truly listening instead of dozing or daydreaming!) may nod their heads in assent, raise their eyebrows in wonder, or clench their teeth in disagreement. But when people are involved in a discussion they are challenged to formulate and possibly even defend their own positions on an issue rather than merely accept or reject the position of the speaker. Furthermore, as discussion continues, the discussion members help each other clarify their values and positions on issues through the give and take of the conversation.

Discussion develops questioning skills. As you will discover later in this handbook, the skilled use of questions is indispensable to leading a meaningful discussion. When people are exposed to a question/answer format during discussion, they learn to investigate, analyze, and apply biblical material through the use of questions. Once learned, the art of asking questions is an invaluable tool in personal and group Bible study.

Discussion creates a sense of community. Just as with any task which requires more than one person for completion, discussion tends to pull people together in the accomplishment of a common goal. A discussion topic or problem becomes *our* topic or problem, the discoveries become *our* discoveries, and the solutions become *our* solutions. A discussion concludes with the awareness that the discoveries and conclusions could not have been reached by the participants working alone, but only by the group process.

Furthermore, Bible discussion encourages group members to open up to one another. People become more willing to share their concerns, fears and hopes. Walls of defensiveness crumble. Masks are slowly removed as participants reveal their real needs and reach out to meet the needs of others. When properly nourished, such an atmosphere melts people into the *koinonia* oneness which the New Testament encourages.

Discussion affirms each participant. Each individual who takes part in a discussion has the satisfaction of knowing that he or she has contributed to the success of the discussion as a whole. Every contribution to the discussion—a comment, a clarifying question, a personal experience, even a nod or a "hmmm"—is of value. It is a learning experience in which each participant can say, "I took part; I helped make it a success."

Discussion taps into learner experiences. What would you think of an orchestra conductor who assembled a group of skilled musicians with their instruments only to have them listen to him play a solo on his own instrument? What a waste of talent! Yet often in adult learning experiences teachers and leaders perform a similar injustice: limiting the input to the scope of their own education and life experiences while their learners remain passive and silent.

Each learner brings into the discussion circle a rich background of Bible knowledge and a wide range of life experiences. Older adults bring more extensive life experiences to the group. Adults who have been Christians for many years bring greater wisdom and deeper Bible knowledge to the group. Group Bible discussion leaders must take advantage of the valuable resources sitting in the circle by encouraging participants to share what they have learned and experienced in the past. The personal insights and life-related examples which surface during Bible discussion will broaden the application of biblical principles for all participants in the group.

Discussion provides needed feedback. Unless he or she calls for specific response to the presentation, the lecturer has little or no idea what the learners are thinking or feeling. It is one-way communication. But in discussion, the leader is getting continual feedback from the participants because they are answering questions, making comments, and sharing personal experiences on the discussion theme. This kind of feedback not only helps the teacher know where the learners are, but helps the learners articulate facts and feelings which might remain unspoken in a lecture format.

☐ The Role of the Discussion Leader

The discussion leader plays the most vital role in the

success of a Bible discussion. Though he or she must keep a low profile in terms of authority in the group, the discussion leader's preparation and leadership (or lack thereof) will make or break the discussion group. Briefly, the discussion leader's role is to keep the discussion moving, encourage participation, and make sure everyone stays on the subject.

Let's identify the components which fit together to make a successful discussion leader. Don't lose heart if you find that some of these elements are weak or missing from your make-up as a teacher/leader. Remember, discussion leaders are made, not born. Each of these elements is more of a learned skill than a natural trait. There is plenty of room for growth in all of us.

A catalyst. In chemistry a catalyst is a substance which, when added to other chemicals, causes changes to occur rapidly. In Bible discussion, the leader is a catalyst causing interaction to take place between the discussion group members. The leader serves as a subtle catalyst by creating the proper atmosphere for the discussion through personal warmth, openness, and preparation. Once the discussion is underway, the leader keeps things happening by asking questions, posing problems, probing for response, and sparking interaction. The leader keeps the ball rolling in discussion by modeling personal interest in the discussion and by skillfully using the discussion tools at his or her disposal.

A guide. Whenever people are encouraged to participate in open discussion, the possibility of individuals getting off the track and onto tangents is always imminent. The discussion leader must be a gentle but firm guide

25

keeping the discussion centered on the Bible text and discussion focus which have been selected. The leader must be ready to ask, "How does your comment relate to the theme of today's Bible text?" in order to help individuals tie their often tangential comments to the discussion focus. People will tend to resist pressure from the leader to "get off your soap box and back onto the subject." But a skillful leader can accomplish this guidance in a way that encourages participants rather than threatens or stifles them.

A clarifier. Each individual who participates in Bible discussion speaks from his or her own background and frame of reference. And since backgrounds and points of view differ, someone in the discussion circle must be ready to clarify questions and comments so that each person in the group has the maximum opportunity to understand and apply what is being said. Though others in the group may help in clarification, the leader must be prepared to be the group clarifier.

There are two areas in which clarification is critical. First, each discussion question must be clear in the minds of the participants. Therefore, it is helpful for the discussion leader to repeat, and often rephrase, questions which are raised in the group—especially his or her own. When writing questions for a Bible discussion, it's a good idea for the leader to think of two or three different ways of stating the question. Rephrasing the questions will help group members grasp the meaning of each question. Also, when another group member raises a question, the leader should repeat the question in his or her own words in order to clarify it for the other members.

26

Second, it is important that the discussion leader help clarify responses to questions and other comments. The leader can clarify responses in several ways. He or she can summarize a lengthy response into a concise sentence in order to help the group members pull the loose ends of the response together in their own minds. The leader may also rephrase responses into language which may be more common to those in the group. One helpful technique in clarification is to say, "Let me restate what I hear you saying, and then you tell me if I'm hearing correctly." This allows discussion members to clarify their own statements as they hear them verbalized by the leader.

Once the discussion leader is operating as a clarifier in the group, other members will pick up the skill of clarification and assist the leader in keeping the waters clear for everyone during the discussion.

Caution needs to be exercised when the leader serves as clarifier during discussion. The leader must not change the meaning of the responses in eagerness to clarify them. Even if the response is incorrect, the leader must not change the response, but merely make it more clear to the other members. It is likely that, as the leader clarifies an incorrect answer, the group will point out the error.

An affirmer. A key element in the discussion leader's role is the ability and willingness to be an affirmer during the process of group discussion. An affirmer is one who encourages others by recognizing the value in each person and contribution. When discussion participants are affirmed by the leader, they sense that both they and their contributions to the discussion are worthwhile and of value to others. Without affirmation, people are often unsure of

27

their worth to the group, and consequently they may unnecessarily withhold their questions and comments from the discussion.

A discussion leader can affirm group members in several ways. First, a discussion leader affirms by giving attention to each person when he or she is speaking. Eye-to-eye contact, pleasant and inviting facial expressions, and even a slight nod of the head from time to time shows that the leader is interested in what the participant has to say. A simple response of "Thank you," "I appreciate that" or "Good thought" encourages participants by helping them see that what they say is of value to the leader.

Second, a discussion leader can affirm and encourage group members by using their names during the discussion period. "That's a good question, Andy," "Thank you, Dee," and "Lindy, what do you think of what Don had to say?" are some examples of how conscious name-dropping can contribute to the atmosphere of affirmation in the discussion group.

In affirming learners, it is important to keep the focus on the individuals rather than on their contributions. If you praise only the right answers or best responses, participants will be reticent to share, thinking that they might not give an acceptable response. But if you praise all the participants for responding, and guide them to the correct answers in the atmosphere of that affirmation, people will be willing to share their responses more readily.

The leader can affirm a participant even when he or she gives a wrong answer or asks a question which is off the subject. "You've hit upon an interesting idea, Glen," the leader might say, "and I wish we had time to get into that subject now. Could we spend a few minutes after class talking about it?"

Third, the leader can foster an atmosphere of affirmation in group discussion by avoiding all put downs. "That's the silliest answer I've ever heard," "Nice try, dummy, but that's wrong," and "I think Denise's answer is better than yours, Hal" are examples of put downs which can destroy the positive atmosphere which encourages openness and sharing in a discussion. Even friendly little chops can be mistaken for destructive criticism which erodes an individual's self-esteem. Accentuate the positive elements and eliminate the negative. Humorous put downs are not worth the few chuckles they may provoke.

☐ What a Discussion Leader Is *Not*

There are several misconceptions of the discussion leader's role which are detrimental to successful Bible discussions. Though the tendency may be to gravitate toward some of these more familiar roles, they must be shunned as unproductive in the discussion process.

The answer person. Some leaders feel that they are responsible to answer every question which arises during a discussion. They see themselves as resident sources of truth who feel duty-bound to dispense volumes of information to their knowledge-starved pupils. Discussion to them is simply a means of getting the learners to ask the questions which they as leaders are to answer. This kind of attitude can be dangerous to the success of group discussion.

The discussion process operates upon the biblical principle that the meaning of God's Word is as available to the participants as it is to the leader (see 1 John 2:27). God gives insight to the group members just as He gives insight to the discussion leader. This means that the participants in a discussion have as much right to answer questions as the leader. The discussion leader who asserts him- or herself as the supreme answerer will stifle the creativity and insight of the group.

Even when the leader knows the correct answer, it is often more beneficial to withhold the answer for a while than to give it. When the leader, from the benefit of research or experience, gives a quick answer to a question, he or she short-circuits the interaction in the group which may help individuals discover the answers for themselves. One of the golden rules of learning is, "Don't tell learners anything that you can help them discover for themselves." Often a quick answer violates this rule and cheats the learner of the opportunity to solve the problem through the discussion process.

The last word. Similar to the attitude of the answer person, some discussion leaders feel responsible to be the final authority during the discussion. They feel they must refute all wrong doctrine and correct every wrong answer. They cannot endure a discussion which leaves learners in question about a particular point.

A discussion group which is led by a "let me set you straight" leader will soon revert to a lecture audience. "Why should I give my views?" a discussion member might say. "He's going to tell us what he wants us to know anyway. Why waste time and effort to discuss our ideas?"

The discussion leader must present the profile of a co-learner in the discussion group. It is okay if the leader does not know all the answers—in fact, it is better if he or she doesn't. This way the group will see their leader as one who is eager to learn, and as such, one who will listen to and accept their ideas.

Contrary to popular opinion, honest doubt among Bible students is often a healthy sign. It is good for a discussion leader to admit occasionally, "I've never thought of that before. I don't know what the answer is. Let's try to find out together." Such an admission opens a discussion group to exciting Bible study and encourages each individual to participate.

The monopolizer. The discussion leader may have been chosen for the position because he or she has demonstrated outstanding skill as a discussion participant. Therefore, the tendency may be for the discussion leader to be the most skilled "discusser" in the group. However, as leader, the role has changed from that of expert participant. Now the job is not to amaze the group with verbal acumen, but to assist others in developing their discussion skills.

In short, if the leader is going to encourage participation in discussion, he or she must exert discipline and be silent. The discussion leader cannot monopolize the conversation no matter how skilled he or she may be in group discussion. Every statement made by the leader subtracts one statement that could have been made by the group. A wise leader will reduce his or her comments to the absolute minimum and concentrate energy on questions which will stimulate the group to profitable discussion.

☐ Planning a Good Discussion

As mentioned earlier, discussion in adult Bible study is not to be seen as an end in itself. Meaningful Bible discussion must have clear aims or it becomes little more than a pooling of opinion or ignorance.

In general, Bible discussions must be in harmony with the basic goal of learning in Christian education. In Christian education, learning is any change in an individual which contributes to his or her spiritual growth. Therefore, Bible discussion is not to be seen as an activity used merely to fill an hour with Bible-based chatter. Rather, each discussion must be planned to encourage specific steps of spiritual growth in the individual participants.

Select a discussion focus. The first step in planning a discussion is to choose a specific focus. A discussion focus is a theme from the Bible text on which you want your learners to concentrate during the discussion period. For example, if your Bible text is Psalm 23, you may want to lead a discussion in the area of God's care over us as the Good Shepherd. Therefore, your discussion focus may be stated as "The shepherding care of God."

With a specific focus chosen, you will have a guideline by which to keep the discussion on track. So when someone comments on the phrase "the valley of the shadow of death" in Psalm 23:4, your discussion focus of God's shepherding care will serve as a point of reference to help you keep the discussion from going off on a tangent. "How does God show His care over us in the valley of the shadow of death?" you might ask to relate the comment to the theme. Without a discussion focus, the discussion may wander off into any of a dozen subjects. But with a specific theme in mind, you can guide the discussion to a profitable and specific conclusion.

It is important to select only one focus for each discussion even though the discussion text may contain several good discussion themes. There is generally only time enough to consider one major theme effectively in a discussion period. It is best to select one focus and do a comprehensive job of covering that theme than to select two or three themes and jump from one to the other.

Select three aims. Once a discussion focus as been chosen, three specific aims for the discussion participant should be outlined—one to guide the formation of questions in each of the three categories of the discussion: information, explanation, and application. These aims should be carefully worded and written down in terms of what the leader desires the learner to achieve in the three successive stages of the discussion.

The first aim needed is an *information* aim. The information aim specifies which *facts* from the text need to be discussed by the learners. This aim is helpful in making sure the participants are guided to discover what the Scripture *says* about a particular theme. For example, an information aim which is in harmony with the discussion focus for Palm 23 mentioned above might be stated, "Guide learners to identify the terms which describe God as a shepherd." With this aim in mind you will be able to structure questions and comments which will help the discussion participants identify God's shepherd-like, caring qualities.

The second aim needed is an *explanation* aim. Once

they have identified the pertinent facts related to the discussion focus in a Scripture passage, participants need to be guided into a discussion of what the facts *mean*. An explanation aim designates the *concepts* and *values* the leader wants the participants to analyze during the discussion.

An explanation aim in harmony with the focus for Psalm 23 might be stated, "Guide learners to explain specific characteristics of God's shepherding care." With this aim before you, your group will have a track to follow in exploring the meaning of Psalm 23.

In addition to an information aim and an explanation aim, each discussion needs an *application* aim. The application aim zeroes in on the personal response individuals can make to the Bible passage. By including an application aim in the discussion plan, you will help each participant assess the value of God's Word in his or her own life.

An example of an application aim based on the Psalm 23 focus previously mentioned is, "Guide learners to identify one area of their lives in which they need to be aware of God's shepherding care this week."

Without an application aim in mind, the discussion leader may leave the group to themselves to bridge the gap between the Bible's meaning and their own response to it. But a specific application aim, and the questions which an application aim dictates, will lead learners to apply to their own lives the truths of Scripture which they discovered during the discussion.

If preparing a Bible discussion was compared to building a house, identifying the focus and specifying the aims would be the same as laying the foundation. Once the house is completed the foundation is virtually invisible and all attention is turned toward the superstructure and furnishings. Yet the beauty and security of the walls and roof would be tenuous at best without the strength of the foundation.

Once the foundation of the Bible discussion is laid (focus and aims), attention must be turned to the visible walls and roof (the questions you will ask). Your discussion group will probably not be aware of the foundation of the discussion. You alone will know of the underlying strength of your preselected focus and aims. But the quality of the discussion questions your learners will hear from you will make all the difference in the success or failure of the Bible study from their viewpoint.

Part Two:

Preparing the
Questions

Ever since men and women discovered their capacity to speak, they have used the question as the prime tool for evoking a response from fellow humans. Socrates was famous for his use of questions in drawing wisdom out of common folk. Jesus was a master at the use of the question. "Who do people say I am?" (Mark 8:27); "Who do you say I am?" (Mark 8:29); "Which of these three do you think was a neighbor to the man who fell into the hands of robbers?" (Luke 10:36).

Questions are an indispensable ingredient in effective discussions, and the art of questioning is an important and necessary discussion leading skill which can be learned and improved upon with practice.

In order to prepare the participants for the discussion questions, they need to become acquainted with the Scripture text to be discussed. Even if the discussion group has been asked to read the passage at home in preparation for the discussion, it is good to reread the section just before the first question is asked.

There are several ways to read a Scripture passage with a group. Have the leader or another prepared reader from the class read the passage aloud while others follow along in their Bibles. Or, if all members have access to the same version, have the class read the section aloud together. Another way is to have prepared class members read the section dramatically. Or, ask two or three people to read the section from different versions of the Bible. It is important to use a variety of approaches in Scripture reading to keep this part of the discussion alive and interesting for participants.

There are three levels of questions which should be

employed in Bible discussion. The three levels of questions correspond with the three aims of Bible discussion mentioned earlier—information, explanation, and application.

☐ Information Questions

An *information* question requires the learner to remember specific facts in order to answer. Information questions invite learners to discuss the what, who, where and when of the passages. When did this event take place? Who was involved in the story? What city were the apostles visiting? The answer to information questions must be available in the Bible text or other information which the learners have immediately at hand. Every learner should have an equal opportunity to answer information questions because the information is equally available to all.

The following information questions are based on the discussion focus and information aim for Psalm 23 which was mentioned earlier. Notice that each question can be answered from the Bible text.

☐ In what occupational role does David see God in Psalm 23? *(Shepherd.)*

☐ What terms in Psalm 23 help emphasize the comparison of God to a good shepherd? *(Pastures, waters, paths, rod, staff, oil, etc.)*

☐ What verbs in Psalm 23 describe God's action

as a good shepherd? *(Lie down, leads, guides, comfort, prepare, etc.)*

It is important to begin a discussion with a few information questions for several reasons. First, it gives every participant an equal opportunity to contribute and thus encourages sharing. At this level, no question is too difficult for anyone since the answers are plainly visible to everyone who holds a Bible. Second, information questions insure that the discussion begins on a solidly biblical foundation. This is the necessary first step to discovering what God's Word means and how it applies to life today.

When learners have difficulty in answering information questions, the questioner may direct their attention to specific verses where the answers to information questions will be found. For example, if the question, "What verbs in Psalm 23 describe God in terms of a shepherd?" is only partially answered in the initial responses, the questioner may ask, "What verbs are found in verse 4?" This gives participants every opportunity to answer the questions instead of being told the answers.

Answers to information questions should be relatively easy for your discussion participants to discover. As such, some members of your group may think that question-and-answer at this stage is somewhat unnecessary, even juvenile. Yet every Bible student comes to the discussion circle with a different level of knowledge. Bible information which is commonplace to one may be brand new to another. For the sake of the least informed in your group, simple information questions are the best place to start.

In order to disarm the "spiritual giants" who may think

you are insulting their intelligence with childish information questions, begin the discussion by saying something like, "This passage may be familiar to some and new to others. I'd like to begin with a few simple questions to help us all start on the same level. The information we share will be good review for all of us."

Remember that the purpose of information questions is not to explore every shred of data in the passage. The discussion focus and information aim will dictate just how much information needs to be illuminated in order to move confidently toward the explanation and, more importantly, the application of the passage to each learner's life. Often, two or three simple information questions will sufficiently launch the discussion into the meaning of the passage.

The following is a broad sample of information questions. Notice how each question requires the participants to explore the Bible passage to discover the correct answer:

☐ From the temptation of Jesus (Matt. 4:1-11)
   What force led Jesus into the wilderness?
   How long did Jesus go without food?
   What were Satan's three temptations?

☐ From the love chapter (1 Cor. 13:1-13)
   What spiritual gifts are useless without love?
   What does love do and not do?
   When will love pass away?

☐ From the faith chapter (Heb. 11:1-40)
   What is the author's definition of faith?

Who were examples of faith and how was their
faith demonstrated?
What is the relationship between faith and pleasing
God?

☐ From the description of the cities of refuge (Josh.
20:1-9)
What was the purpose of the cities of refuge?
Where were the cities of refuge located?
Whose idea was it to designate cities of refuge?

☐ Explanation Questions

The second level of questions, *explanation* questions,
lead the discussion participants into dialog on the meaning
of the Bible passage under discussion. Explanation questions require learners to analyze the facts they have verbalized during the information section of the discussion in
terms of the concepts and principles which are to be found
there. During the explanation stage of the discussion,
learners are synthesizing information in the Bible text—
and in parallel Scriptures which may be introduced in the
course of the discussion—into biblical principles which
apply to life today.

In the case of explanation questions, answers may not
be found specifically in the Bible narrative, but may be
implied in the content of the text. For example, an explanation question which may be included in the discussion of
the shepherding care of God from Psalm 23 might be,
"What do these verses teach you about the nature of
God?" The answers which may be given—that God is a

loving, caring, disciplining guide—do not appear verbatim in the six verses of Psalm 23. But the descriptive words which *do* appear in the text—"I shall lack nothing," "He leads me," "rod and staff," etc.—imply that God is by nature a loving, caring, disciplining guide. That correct analysis can be substantiated by parallel Scriptures. The resourceful discussion leader will guide learners to supportive Scriptures which validate their discoveries during the explanation phase of the discussion.

During the explanation section of a discussion, it is possible that some learners may suggest an incorrect analysis from the Scripture portion. This possibility will be minimized when the information level questions have thoroughly prepared the discussion group for analysis.

In the event of an incorrect answer, ask clarifying questions to help the learner identify how he or she arrived at the conclusion. For example, the question "How did you arrive at that conclusion?" will provoke the learner to retrace his or her thinking and perhaps discover the fault in logic. Often other members of the discussion group will see the fault and point it out. This is desirable because it keeps the burden of authority on the group rather than on you the leader. A more thorough treatment of the subject of wrong responses during discussion will be presented in Part Three of this handbook.

When you ask people to explain the meaning of a certain text, quotation or event from Scripture, be prepared to accept a variety of responses. Some learners will deduce from the passage the same meaning you have found. But others may arrive at some different yet equally valid conclusions which you have overlooked. Your ability to sit in the discussion group as a leader *and* a learner will prepare you to welcome new discoveries which were not on your "script" for the discussion.

Other learners will offer good answers which are not pertinent to the topic under discussion. Each time a discussion slips off track, you must decide whether or not the new topic verbalized is of sufficient value to the group to abandon your planned discussion focus. If not, tactfully thank the contributor for his or her thought, then return to the central theme you have selected.

Again, it is not necessary to exhaust the meaning of a Bible passage during the explanation phase of discussion. There will almost always be more to talk about than you have time for if you attempt to pose every conceivable explanation question. Rather, write two to four explanation questions which will draw your learners to the heart of the passage. Avoid the temptation to consider every main point in favor of centering on one main point for the discussion.

In the following sample of explanation questions, notice how learners are challenged to discuss the meaning of the various passages:

☐ From the resurrection of Jesus (John 19:38—20:31)

Why did Jesus prevent Mary Magdalene from touching Him?

Should Thomas be chastised for his doubt? Why or why not?

☐ From Jesus' statements on prayer (Matt. 6:5-15)

Why is it important to pray in secret?

If God knows what we need before we ask, why do we need to pray?

What is the importance of forgiveness in relation to prayer?

☐ From Paul's statements on the church as the Body of Christ (1 Cor. 12:12-31)

What do you think it means to "drink" of the Spirit?

Who are the weaker members in a church?

What does it mean to desire the greater gifts?

☐ From Paul's qualities for leadership (1 Tim. 3:1-15)

Why did Paul insist that overseers and deacons be good managers of their families?

Why did Paul designate men and not women for leadership roles?

☐ Application Questions

The third level of questions in discussion are *application* questions. Application questions help learners examine their own values and apply the facts and principles discovered through information and explanation questions to the specifics of their own lives. At the information level, participants discuss teachings, facts, personalities, places and events which happened and were recorded at least twenty centuries ago. At the explanation level, attention shifts to the significance and relevance of the facts and timeless principles found in the passage. But at the application level, questions are specifically framed to help learners apply the information and principles to their own lives today. Application questions personalize the Scriptures to "our" world, "our" church and "our" lives.

There are two distinct stages of application questions and both are valuable in helping people personalize the message of Scripture to their lives. The first stage is *general* application which basically asks, "How are *we* going to apply God's Word to *our* lives?" The second stage is *personal* application which narrows the focus to ask, "How am *I* going to apply God's Word to *my* life?"

The difference between the two stages of application is subtle but very important. At the first stage, each member is safely tucked within the anonymity of the group. The threat and the commitment are at a minimum because each individual is only one of several discussing how "we" (our group, our church, Christians in general) need to respond to the Bible's message. The second stage brings each individual into the spotlight by asking, "How are *you* going to respond?" The generalities of a group response are good but each individual must make personal application of God's Word. Though there may be similarities in response between group members, personal application questions evoke the unique response which represents each person's unique relationship with God.

General application questions will always contain pronouns like *we, us,* and *our.* From the Psalm 23 discussion, a general application question would be, "In what ways are we in need of God's shepherding care today?" An effective

47

personal application question will always contain the word *you* or *your*—"In what area of *your* life do *you* need to be aware of God's shepherding care this week?" Often one or two good application questions from each stage will be sufficient to lead learners to make personal application of the biblical material to their lives. Sometimes a general application question can become a personal application question by simply changing the third person pronouns to first person pronouns. You can effectively use an application question twice by making a simple change of "we" to "me" or "you."

Notice in the following examples that most application questions can be used as general and/or personal application:

☐ From Jesus' crucifixion (Luke 23:26-49)
   How would we have responded if we had watched the crucifixion?
   What do you think Jesus might have said to you from the cross?

☐ From Christ's comparison with the Good Shepherd (John 10:1-21)
   When in your life have you stubbornly rebelled against God's shepherding leadership?
   What are the most important benefits we enjoy from God's shepherding care?

☐ From Jesus' conversation with Nicodemus (John 3:1-21)
   What were the circumstances which accompanied your second birth?

48

If you had been Nicodemus, what might you have asked about being born again?

☐ From John's teaching on forgiveness (1 John 1:5—2:2)
What obstacles stand in our way between unconfessed sin and forgiveness?
For what aspect of forgiveness are you most thankful today?

Caution must be exercised at the personal application stage of the discussion due to the personal nature of the questions. Whereas with information, explanation and general application questions the leader is seeking group response—answers which are common to each member of the group—with personal application questions the leader is eliciting personal responses—answers which are unique to each individual in the group. Some believers are willing to talk unreservedly about their personal responses to Bible discussion, but others are not. Furthermore, some responses may be so deeply personal in nature that sharing them openly in a group would not benefit the individual nor the group.

Say, for example, that your discussion focus was the importance of pure thoughts for believers. If you ask individuals to respond to the personal question, "What areas of your thought life do you need to clean up this week?" you may be setting a match to a powder keg of personal information which needs to remain personal. You would do better to ask a question to which members can respond without embarrassing themselves or the group, such as "What phrase from today's Scripture passage we've discussed do you specially need to put into practice this week?" This question allows each individual to focus on God's specific message to him or her that day without unnecessarily revealing personal information.

Here's a good rule of thumb for all levels of discussion questions, but particularly for questions at the personal level: Always allow members the option of passing (not commenting) on any question which may be asked. Learners need to feel that their responses are welcome, but that no pressure will be placed upon them to participate in the discussion. This may mean that some of your discussion group members will not participate. But it is far better that some remain in the group without commenting than be driven from the group completely by unnecessary pressure. Furthermore, there are positive ways to encourage participation which will not threaten or intimidate learners. Tips for involving non-participants will be discussed later in this handbook.

☐ Sample Discussions

How do all the pieces and parts from the three levels of questions fit together? The next several pages contain numerous examples of completely assembled discussion plans. The focus, aims and questions for each plan fit together to form a solid, biblically based, stimulating plan for leading a Bible discussion. Notice that the questions are derived from the written aims, and the aims are derived from the specific discussion focus.

☐
Sample Discussions

****** Discussion Text: Psalm 23:1-6 ******

Discussion Focus: God cares for us like a good shepherd.

Information Aim: Guide learners to identify the terms which describe God as a shepherd.

Information Questions:

1. In what occupational role does David see God in Psalm 23?

2. What terms in Psalm 23 emphasize the comparison of God to a good shepherd?

3. What verbs in the Psalm describe God's action as a good shepherd?

Explanation Aim: Guide learners to compare the shepherd concepts with the caring traits of God.

Explanation Questions:

1. What do these verses teach you about the nature of God?

2. What do these verses teach you about the nature of man?

3. What other Scripture verses can you think of which reinforce the picture of God as a good shepherd?

Application Aim: Guide learners to select one area of their lives where they need to be aware of God's shepherding care this week.

Application Questions:

1. In what ways are people today in need of God's shepherding care?

2. How has God exercised His shepherding care over your life recently?

3. In what area of your life do you need to be aware of God's shepherding care this week?

* * * * * * * * Discussion Text: James 1:1-8 * * * * * * * *

Discussion Focus: How to handle trials.

Information Aim: Guide learners to list the biblical responses to trials which they encounter.

Information Questions:

1. What ways does James instruct Christians to handle the trials they encounter?

2. What results does James promise when a believer responds to trials correctly?

3. What happens when a person asks for wisdom but does not believe that God will provide it?

Explanation Aim: Guide learners to explain the importance of rejoicing, wisdom and faith in handling trials.

Explanation Questions:

1. Why is it important for a person to rejoice in his trials?

2. Why is it important to ask for wisdom in trials?

3. Why is it important to have faith when asking for wisdom?

Application Aim: Guide learners to describe one trial in their lives which they need to handle in the scriptural way.

Application Questions:

1. What keeps Christians today from rejoicing in trials and asking for wisdom?

2. When have you experienced a trial and made the right responses? What were the results?

3. In what area of your life are you presently facing trials? What responses do you need to make?

******* Discussion Text: Joshua 20:1-9 *******

Discussion Focus: God is our refuge.

Information Aim: Guide learners to define the purpose and function of the cities of refuge.

Information Questions:

1. What was the purpose of the cities of refuge?

2. Whose idea was it to designate cities of refuge?

3. What was the refuge city's responsibility toward the unintentional manslayer?

Explanation Aim: Guide learners to compare the function of the cities of refuge with the refuge offered to believers in God today.

Explanation Questions:

1. What does the establishment of the cities of refuge suggest about the nature of God?

2. How was the geographic location of the six cities a benefit to the people?

3. How do the cities of refuge compare to the refuge we find in God?

Application Aim: Guide learners to determine the aspect of God's refuge they need in their lives today.

Application Questions:

1. What are some areas of life today from which believers need refuge?

2. In what ways has God provided refuge for you personally?

3. Would someone be willing to share an area where you feel a need for God's refuge today?

****** Discussion Text: 1 John 1:5—2:2 ******

Discussion Focus: Forgiveness of sins is available to all through Jesus Christ.

Information Aim: Guide learners to identify John's description of sin and God's plan for forgiveness.

Information Questions:

1. What metaphor did John use to describe God?

2. What is the result of walking in God's light?

3. What role do Christians play in receiving forgiveness of sins?

4. What role does God play?

Explanation Aim: Guide learners to explain the need for forgiveness in light of God's provision.

Explanation Questions:

1. What does the darkness in this passage symbolize?

2. What does it mean to walk in God's light?

3. If God purifies Christians from all unrighteousness, why do they still sin?

Application Aim: Guide learners to confess sin in their lives and receive God's forgiveness.

Application Questions:

1. What keeps us from confessing sin and receiving forgiveness?

2. What phrase from this passage is most meaningful to you and why?

3. What area of darkness in your life needs to be confessed and forgiven today?

* * * * * * Discussion Text: Matthew 6:5-15 * * * * * *

Discussion Focus: Following the guidelines for prayer and reaping the benefits of prayer.

Information Aim: Guide learners to identify the do's and don'ts for prayer.

Information Questions:

1. What are the do's of prayer mentioned in this passage?

2. What are the don'ts of prayer?

3. What is the reward for the secret prayer?

Explanation Aim: Guide learners to explain the significance of the Lord's prayer.

Explanation Questions:

1. Why is it important and beneficial to pray in secret?

2. How can Christians pray for each other without drawing attention to themselves?

3. What does this passage teach about the frequency of personal prayer?

Application Aim: Guide learners to evaluate their own prayer lives and plan specific ways to improve.

Application Questions:

1. Where and when do you pray?

2. How does your prayer life measure up to Jesus' teaching in these verses?

3. What one thing from this Scripture could you do this week to improve your prayer life?

****** Discussion Text: Galatians 6:1-10 ******

Discussion Focus: Biblical principles for restoring a sinning Christian to fellowship in the church.

Information Aim: Guide learners to identify the biblical pattern for confronting Christians in sin.

Information Questions:

1. Who does Paul say should restore sinning Christians?

2. What warnings does Paul give to those who would restore a sinning Christian?

Explanation Aim: Guide learners to determine practical steps for restoring sinning Christians.

Explanation Questions:

1. Who are the "spiritual" ones Paul suggests should initiate restoration? How does one know whether or not he is spiritual?

2. How would someone heed Paul's warnings to guard against falling?

63

3. What are some elements which might be included in the process of restoration?

Application Aim: Guide learners to identify their level of preparation for the ministry of restoration.

Application Questions:

1. Why is it difficult for Christians to confront each other concerning sin?

2. What do you find most difficult about the thought of confrontation?

3. On a scale of one to ten, how prepared are you to reach out to a sinning believer?

4. What needs to happen in your life to better prepare you for restoration?

****** Discussion Text: Nehemiah 8:1-8 ******

Discussion Focus: Reverence for God and His Word.

Information Aim: Guide learners to identify ways Israel expressed reverence for God and His Word.

Information Questions:

1. What conditions were provided for the people to express reverence for God and His Word?

2. What specific words and actions did the people employ to express their reverence?

Explanation Aim: Guide learners to determine the value of specific words and actions of reverence.

Explanation Questions:

1. How do the downward postures of bowing and kneeling express reverence to God?

2. How do the upward postures of standing and lifting hands express reverence to God?

3. Why is it important to express inward reverence through outward behavior?

Application Aim: Guide learners to implement expressions of reverence to God in their own lives.

Application Questions:

1. How could some of the expressions of reverence in this passage be employed in personal worship?

2. How do you feel about expressing reverence and worship through physical postures such as kneeling or lifting hands?

3. What specific expression of reverence would you choose to exercise in the coming week?

***** Discussion Text: 2 Corinthians 9:6-15 *****

Discussion Focus: The benefits and results of biblical giving.

Information Aim: Guide learners to identify the biblical motivation behind Christian giving.

Information Questions:

1. What are the proper and improper motivations for giving that Paul outlined in this passage?

2. What benefits are promised to those who give from proper motivation?

3. What are the results of Christian giving beyond the benefits enjoyed by the giver?

Explanation Aim: Guide learners to discuss the limitless boundaries of Christian giving.

Explanation Questions:

1. Why do you think Paul omitted any mention of the tithe in this passage?

2. What are the guidelines by which Christians should decide how much to give and to whom to give?

3. What guidelines should be followed as to *what* Christians may give (money, food, etc.)?

Application Aim: Guide learners to expose themselves to the benefits of giving by taking a new step in their personal commitment to give.

Application Questions:

1. Why is it often difficult for Christians to find room in their budgets for generous giving?

2. What giving philosophy do you follow?

3. What one step can you take in the coming week to apply Paul's advice to your giving?

****** Discussion Text: Galatians 5:13-26 ******

Discussion Focus: The fruit of the Spirit should be evident in the life of every believer.

Information Aim: Guide learners to contrast the fruit of the Spirit with the acts of the sinful nature.

Information Questions:

1. How can Christians avoid fulfilling the desires of the flesh?

2. What does the sinful nature desire?

3. Which acts of the sinful nature would be obliterated by love? Joy? The other fruits of the Spirit?

Explanation Aim: Guide learners to verbalize the importance of expressing the fruit of the Spirit in everyday life.

Explanation Questions:

1. What does Paul mean by the statement, "Those who live like this (acts of the sinful nature) will not inherit the kingdom of God"?

2. How do Christians consciously shun the sinful nature and embrace the fruit of the Spirit?

3. If the believer's sinful nature is crucified with Christ, why do Christians still sin?

Application Aim: Guide learners to select one fruit of the Spirit they would like to see grow in their lives in the coming week.

Application Questions:

1. Which fruit of the Spirit do you think Christians have the greatest difficulty expressing?

2. Which fruit of the Spirit seems to be most lacking in your life?

3. What actions will you take this week to encourage the development of a lacking fruit of the Spirit in your life?

* * * * * * Discussion Text: Philippians 2:1-11 * * * * * *

Discussion Focus: Christians are to imitate Christ's humility.

Information Aim: Guide learners to define humility from Christ's example.

Information Questions:

1. What specific words from this passage suggest that Christ exhibited the attitude of humility?

2. What is humility according to this passage?

3. What specific actions of humility does Paul encourage for Christians?

Explanation Aim: Guide learners to illustrate the expression of Christ's humility in today's culture.

Explanation Questions:

1. What does it mean to "consider others better than yourselves"?

2. What might Christ's example of humility look like in the life of a present-day Christian?

Application Aim: Guide learners to determine ways they can imitate Christ's attitude of humility in daily life.

Application Questions:

1. When is the characteristic of humility most difficult for you to exercise?

2. What are some ways you could make yourself "nothing" in Christ's example?

3. What is the most helpful concept from this passage for you?

☐ Helpful Tips

Here are a few additional tips for getting the most discussion mileage out of your information, explanation and application questions.

Plan questions in advance. The most successful discussions are not spontaneous; they are carefully planned. It is to your advantage as a discussion leader to write down your discussion focus, aims, and questions in the sequence in which you will use them. Written questions insure that your discussion will stay on track. You may think of additional questions during the course of the discussion, but your planned sequence will provide you a secure framework of reference.

Avoid questions which can be answered yes or no. Questions of this nature do not promote discussion, they stifle it. Discussion questions should provoke members to explain, illustrate, defend, or clarify a biblical principle. A yes or no answer accomplishes none of these tasks. A yes or no type question is only appropriate when it is followed by "Why?" or "Why not?"

Refer to your notes. Once you have written focus, aims, and questions, transfer the questions to a small card or sheet of paper which will fit compactly into your Bible. It will be easier for you and less distracting for your class members if you follow a concise outline of questions than if you fumble through a sheaf of notes. You need not be embarrassed about using notes to lead a discussion. You and your learners will discover that following a guideline to achieve productivity in discussion far outweighs whatever value the appearance of spontaneity may hold.

Part Three:

Handling the Problems

Have you ever evaluated the group discussion process with a sentence which began something like, "Group Bible discussions would be great if only . . . "? Perhaps you uttered your comment with a sigh of disappointment or disillusionment, a snarl of anger or even a whimper of defeat. And you may have completed your evaluative statement in several ways, like, "some people would talk more," "some people would talk less," "some people would stay on the subject," or "some people would avoid arguing, preaching or pushing their own pet doctrine."

Let's face it: group discussion invites a lot of problems and they are almost always people problems. That's where the lecture method appears to have a great advantage. The lecture-oriented teacher loads up on lesson material during personal study and simply unloads during the Bible study while the "audience" sits there like a collection of cassette recorders. No arguments, no "off the wall" comments or questions, no hassles trying to open up some people and shut up others.

But for reasons already outlined in Part One, the discussion method of group Bible study offers far more advantages to individual students than the potential problems it poses to the leader. When you invite people to open their mouths you're never sure what will come out. But the value of the group discussion process in promoting thought, interaction and commitment is worth the risk of problems.

Since we choose not to avoid discussion problems by shelving the valuable discussion method, our approach to the difficulties encountered becomes one of preventing and solving rather than escaping. Discussion problems must be viewed as challenges to be conquered rather than threats to be feared. We anticipate the obstacles standing between us and a successful discussion much like a hurdler anticipates the hurdles he or she must clear in order to reach the finish line. The rewards of reaching the goal stimulate us to aggressively prepare for and surmount momentary impediments.

The tips which follow might easily be categorized into two sections headed, "A pound of prevention" and "an ounce of cure." Since many potential problems in group discussion can be averted by careful planning, the first two tips deal with preventative measures. The leader's thoughtful attention to pre-session preparation will calm the waters for relatively smooth sailing during the discussion and keep mid-course problem-solving to a minimum. The preventative tips are followed by several suggested "cures" for often unforeseen problems which may arise during the progress of the discussion.

☐ How to Start and Stop

The effectiveness of a Bible discussion can be increased when the leader knows how to get the discussion started and how to bring the discussion to a meaningful conclusion. Special care must be taken that participants are invited into the discussion atmosphere in a way which makes them want to participate. Furthermore, the discussion must conclude in a manner which helps the individual gain the most personal value from the discussion. Therefore it is suggested that each discussion have as its bookends an approach activity and a conclusion activity.

78

Approach. The objective of an approach activity is to help the participants focus their attention on the theme of the discussion. The approach activity serves as a buffer between the arrival of the participants and the first information question. It acclimates the discussion group to the basic subject matter of the topic they will be discussing from the discussion text.

An approach activity (approximately five minutes in duration) can be as simple as a question or as involved as a brief creative assignment. For example, here are some approach activities which could be used to introduce a discussion of God's shepherding care from Psalm 23:

☐ Ask the group to imagine that they are sheep and answer the question, "What are the qualities of a good shepherd?"

☐ Prearrange a staged interview with one of the group members as David. Ask him to compare the skills of a shepherd to God's shepherding care.

☐ Give each individual a sheet of blank paper and ask them to draw on it a symbol that represents "caring" to them.

☐ Discuss the following question in circle response (each person speaks once around the circle without interruption by others): "What do you think of when you hear the word *caring?*"

Notice how each approach activity leads into a Bible discussion of Psalm 23 and God's shepherding care. By the time the approach activity has concluded, each member's interest is aroused and each is ready to dig into the Word for some biblical principles.

Conclusion. What do you do after the last personal application question has been asked? How do you wrap up the discussion in a meaningful way for each participant? One way is by planning a brief conclusion activity to help each group member make specific application of the principles which were explored and discovered during the discussion. The conclusion activity helps each person answer the question, "What am I going to do with what I've learned?"

A conclusion activity may range from a brief prayer in pairs or threes to outlining a project which is to be followed up during the succeeding week. Here are some conclusion activities which could be used effectively to wrap up the discussion of God's shepherding care from Psalm 23:

☐ Have the group gather in clusters of three and pray for each other, particularly for the areas in their lives in which they need God's care today.

☐ Give each person a sheet of paper and pencil. Invite everyone to write a letter of thanks to God for the element of His shepherding care which they appreciate most.

☐ Give each person a small index card. Instruct each member to write on the index card a prayer request regarding God's care over him or her in the coming week. Collect the cards and put them in a coffee can. Each person then draws out of the can a prayer request to remember in the coming week.

With a little bit of thought, the leader can create a brief conclusion activity to help each learner draw some personal conclusion and designate some personal responses to what he or she has learned during the discussion. Other creative approach and conclusion activities can be found in the book *How to Do Bible Learning Activities—Adult* (Ventura, California: Gospel Light Publications, 1982).

☐ The Environmental Impact

You've developed sound skills for leading discussions. You've written solid aims. Your questions go right to the point of the Scripture passage to be studied. You are ready to face the challenge of leading a group of adults in a discussion of God's shepherding care as seen in Psalm 23. Or are you?

One element remains. Receptivity for discussion is greatly influenced by the environment which establishes an "atmosphere" or "feel" for the discussion. Many factors contribute to the environment for discussion. Here are a few.

Space. Although little "action" may take place during a discussion, adults still need ample room. Twenty adults in a small apartment might facilitate a feeling of warmth and closeness at first. However, after half an hour or so the feeling of warmth becomes one of stuffiness. Closeness becomes claustrophobia.

Room size and availability may force you to limit the size of the discussion group. This is more than acceptable, since the optimum size of a discussion group is about a dozen people.

Lighting and ventilation. It is important that your discussion facilities have proper lighting, heating, cooling, and ventilation. All of these factors contribute to the overall effect. When the room is well-lit and at the proper temperature, learners feel comfortable enough to participate. When participants are physically uncomfortable they are more easily distracted or irritated during the Bible study. Care for these physical needs ahead of time and you will solve potential problems before they arise.

Noise-level. Nothing can stop a discussion faster than a noisy distraction—a crying baby, a police siren, loud neighbors. To the best of your ability, try to insure that the outside world will not invade your group during the discussion. In a home setting this may mean unplugging the phone, providing child care, or turning off the TV or stereo. For a classroom this might suggest closing the door to a noisy hallway.

Seating arrangement. Small circles of moveable chairs are best for a discussion. The circular arrangement tells participants that everyone is equal; all opinions are welcome. Moveable chairs are helpful when you want to break the discussion group into pairs or clusters of three or four for special assignments.

Refreshments. There's something almost magical about the way a cup of coffee, tea or punch opens people up to conversation. It's as if the availability of liquid refreshment—whether it is imbibed or not—lubricates the larynx, promoting verbal interaction. Add to the beverages a plate of snacks and the setting becomes almost festive.

In a group discussion format, refreshments most always promote the atmosphere of fellowship and conversation which encourages the discussion process. Sometimes a Bible study associated with a meal is an additional benefit. Breakfasts, luncheons and dinners, and their attending interaction, help build relationships which are profitable to the openness that the discussion circle solicits.

Refreshments need not always be the responsibility of the leader. Invite group members to supply snacks and beverages on a rotating basis. If the study group meets around a full meal, vary the responsibility for the meal between group members as hosts and perhaps a no-host meeting at a local restaurant.

Only when you've considered the impact of the environment upon your discussion group members are you truly prepared to lead a discussion.

☐ When Nobody Responds

Once adequate preparations have been made and your discussion group is seated with their Bibles open, one of the most common problems is non-participation. You ask what you think is a thought-provoking question and receive nothing but blank stares, as if your group has suddenly turned into statues. The silence tempts you to abandon the discussion and begin filling the void with teacher talk.

There are several reasons why a discussion question may draw a blank response from your group. In each case there are steps which can be taken to remedy the situation.

Participants may be unfamiliar with the discussion format. Many adult Bible students are more familiar and comfortable with the teacher doing most of the talking in a Bible study. These people come with a mind set which says, "The teacher did all the studying and knows all the answers. Who am I to clutter his wise words with my insignificant comments?" As much as you may discourage it, your learners may project onto you the role of the fountain of truth from whom they are ready only to receive, not to give.

If group discussion is new to most of your learners, you may want to acclimate them slowly by offering a blend of question-and-answer and teacher lecture at first. As they become more comfortable with the group discussion process, more of your statements can be replaced by questions.

The meaning of the question may be unclear. It is a good idea to ask, "Is my question clear?" if the question is greeted by blank stares or silence. Be ready to rephrase the question to help participants grasp exactly what you are wanting them to deal with.

84

Participants may need time to think. The leader may have discovered several good answers to the question posed during his or her personal research. But the participants have just heard the question for the first time! They need time to assess what they think and how they will respond.

The leader can reassure the group during silence by saying, "Think about it for a moment and I'll wait for your response." When learners know that silence is not a threat to the leader, they will be more relaxed about taking a few seconds to think through their answers.

Some participants may be shy about speaking in a group. Make sure that group members know that they are not required to participate in the discussion. With the atmosphere of voluntary participation, there are several ways the leader can encourage even shy learners to take part in the discussion. One way is to announce, "We'd really like to have everyone's responses and ideas on this subject. Your ideas may help us understand more. Who else will share at this point?"

Another way is to watch for body language which suggests that participants want to inject a comment but may need a little coaxing. A person leaning forward, a slightly open mouth, a furrowed brow, or nod of the head may indicate a desire to say something. The leader may encourage the shy learner through eye-to-eye contact, a warm smile, and perhaps the question, "Were you about to share something, Terry?"

Another way to deal with a shy participant is to speak to him or her encouragingly in private. "Pat, I know you are a thoughtful person and I am sure you have some good ideas. I think the group would like to hear them. How can I encourage you to share your thoughts with us?"

☐ When Someone Monopolizes

Occasionally a discussion group is frustrated and annoyed by an individual who has a comment (or series of comments) for every question or point of discussion. The comments may be good, but he or she short-circuits the contributions of other members by talking incessantly. Such a person may have a need for recognition which is easily met by the convenience of the discussion group. Whatever the reason, the discussion group suffers if this need for attention, recognition, or esteem in the eyes of others takes precedence over the success of the group experience.

There are several ways of handling the excessive talker in the discussion group. Since his or her talking in the group often reveals a need for attention to some degree, it is important that these suggestions be carried out with plenty of consideration and "tender loving care."

Give general group guidelines for participation. The leader can often alleviate the problem of one excessive talker by making general instructions to the discussion group about how individuals should participate. The leader might announce, "In order to give everyone an opportunity to participate in the discussion, let's operate under the general rule that no one can speak twice on a point until everyone else in the group has been given the opportunity to speak once." Make sure that you couch the announcement in language which is not offensive to the individual you are trying to restrain.

Enlist the offender's aid in the group. Another way to solve the problem is to ask the excessive talker to help you involve the others in the group. In private the leader might say, "Leslie, you have very good ideas to share during our discussions and you seem to feel quite free about expressing them. Sometimes others in the group hold back waiting for you to speak. You could help me involve the others by holding back yourself until some of the others have spoken. Perhaps you could even encourage them to share their ideas. It would be very helpful to me if you could do that."

Confront the problem person straight on. When all else fails, the leader must confront the offender directly about the problem he or she is causing in the group. The individual must be told lovingly but firmly that he or she is taking discussion time away from other members through excessive participation. Request that he or she cooperate with the goals of group discussion by limiting the contributions made and by encouraging the participation of others. Such a confrontation is often difficult for the group leader. But the health and success of the discussion group must take precedence over the undisciplined member. When subtler methods fail, it is imperative that individuals be dealt with.

☐ When an Answer Is Irrelevant

Be careful that you do not judge a statement as being "off track" too quickly. The comment may be relevant to the topic at hand to everyone but you! The main objective for the leader is to understand what the learner meant by the comment and how it relates to the discussion topic.

Affirm the contributor. Always make a point to thank the speaker for the comment in an affirmative way. "That is an interesting thought; I've never thought of that before." The trick is to affirm the participant without encouraging the tangential subject he or she wants to discuss.

seems insincere

Relate the comment to the discussion theme. After expressing affirmative words for the contributor, the leader must establish a link between the comment and the discussion theme and pull the discussion back on track. The most direct approach is to ask, "Would you help us see how your comment relates to the theme of our discussion today?" If the comment is irrelevant to the discussion, the contributor will often admit so in response to the question. If the comment *is* relevant, the leader's question will open the door for the comment to become relevant to the rest of the group.

Another way to relate the "off track" comment to the theme is for the leader to rephrase the comment in terms which pull the group's thinking back on the discussion track. For example, if the discussion focus is God's shepherding care and someone injects a comment about wanting to quit his job, the leader might say, "There are many times in our lives, like the experience which Bryan has just described, where we need to be aware of God's care for us in spite of circumstances. That brings us back to Psalm 23."

The other members in the discussion group can often assist you in getting the discussion back on track after an irrelevant comment or question. The leader can take advantage of the group by asking something like,

"Dorothy, would you respond to Eileen's comment in light of what we have been discussing?" Hopefully some of the class members will be able to see a way to tie the "off track" statement into the discussion theme or help you kindly dismiss it as irrelevant to the topic.

Be alert to a Spirit-led "right turn." The discussion leader should come to the group "prayed up" and confident that the Holy Spirit has prepared him or her for the session. But there are times when a seemingly irrelevant comment can be a signal to the leader that a more important topic needs to be discussed. For example, a group member mentions the death of an unbelieving family member, doubting the validity of prayers for that loved one's salvation. Other group members immediately lean forward and voice similar comments and questions which threaten to derail the planned discussion topic. The leader has the option of making a hard "right turn" to follow the injected topic or tactfully dragging the group back to the original theme. At such a moment of decision, the leader must rely on the Holy Spirit's guidance and be ready to respond to it.

A "right turn" during the discussion is always possible, but will be the exception rather than the rule. The discussion leader who finds that every planned discussion ends up on the scrap heap in favor of the group's "hot buttons" will need to reassess the overall purpose of the group meeting. If the group gathers for specific, life-changing Bible study, the leader must assume his or her role as guide to help the group reach a meaningful conclusion.

☐ When an Answer Is Wrong

First we must define a wrong answer. A wrong answer

to an information question is fairly easy to spot: the Bible text gives specific information and answers are recognizable as wrong or right from the text. For example, if your information question is, "How many cities of refuge did God instruct Joshua to establish?" and someone answers, "Five," the Bible text enumerating *six* cities of refuge proves that answer to be wrong.

But for explanation questions an answer may be more a matter of biblical interpretation, and as such, not as easy to declare right or wrong. Wrong answers would most easily be identified as those which contradict church doctrine or established interpretation of Scripture.

Furthermore, a wrong answer for an explanation question may be one which does not focus on the discussion theme. Say, for example, the discussion focus is again God's shepherding care and the explanation question is, "What do these verses teach you about the nature of God?" If a participant responds by saying, "This teaches me that God is a God of judgment because He uses a rod," the answer may be technically correct, but it does not chime in with the discussion focus of God's shepherding care. In a sense, then, the answer is wrong.

A wrong answer for questions at the application level is even more difficult to identify. The nature of the personal application question is such that the participants must find an answer which is right for themselves. The standard for right or wrong is the individual and God's personal message to him or her during a Bible discussion. For example, if the question is "In what area of your life do you need to be aware of God's shepherding care this week?" it is conceivable that each individual will have a different answer—

all of them being right.

There are several good ways of responding to a wrong answer and guiding learners to correct answers. Again, it is of the utmost importance to affirm the learner for contributing to the discussion. If the leader's response suggests, "That was a dumb answer," it is unlikely that the individual will want to respond again.

Ask the participant to retrace his or her steps. One way to handle a wrong answer during discussion is to encourage the individual to explain how he or she arrived at the conclusion. The leader's question might sound something like this: "Your response interests me. How did you happen to come to that conclusion?" Often in the course of explaining the logic, a person will discover the erroneous thinking, or another member of the group will point it out.

If it is an information question, the person with the wrong answer needs to be redirected to the Scripture passage for correction. The leader might say, "Let's see how the verse puts it" or "Let's see how our text explains it, making sure we understand."

If the wrong response is given to an explanation question, the learner needs to explain to the group how he or she derived the concepts or principles from the text at hand or supplementary material.

Ask the participant to research his or her response. If the discussion member gives a wrong answer which he or she cannot document, the leader might suggest that the group keep the answer "on the back burner" until the answering participant (and/or other group members) can do some research to validate the response. The issue can be quickly resolved during a subsequent meeting as the researchers present their findings. Usually, they will have uncovered their erroneous thinking and will be ready to admit it.

Do some personal research on the erroneous point. If the wrong answer or comment is of such a serious nature that it requires the leader's personal attention, he or she might do research on the issue and bring back a report. The leader might respond, "That is an interesting comment and I'm not sure I know how to respond. I would like to do some studying on that point in order to respond more intelligently to what you said."

It is practically impossible for the leader to be prepared to correct every wrong comment. Furthermore, if the leader accepted the role of the "ultimate authority" in the group by correcting every erroneous idea, the group would soon "clam up" and let the leader do all the talking. "Why should I risk the embarrassment of giving an answer which may be wrong," your learners will think, "when the leader is going to tell us what to think anyway?"

A discussion leader should study thoroughly and prepare for many points of view. But rather than squash every wrong or different view with his authoritative comments, a good leader will use questions and affirmation to assist the group in discovering the truth—and bringing to light any error—for themselves.

☐ When Participants Disagree

One of the risks of opening discussion to a group is the possibility of disagreement among some of the group members. Someone will express an opinion on a topic and someone else will say, "I disagree with that. I believe this way." A disagreement between two or more group members can delay the progress of the discussion and cause other group members to feel left out until the disagreement is settled. Therefore it is important for the group leader to remedy the situation quickly so that the group can continue toward the discussion focus.

Clarify the issues in disagreement. Many disagreements are primarily a matter of semantics. One member disagrees with another's way of stating a point, but in reality they are in agreement on the issue itself. In such a case, the leader needs to ask, "Elaine, what did you hear Steven saying? Would you summarize what you heard in your own words?" When Elaine summarizes what she heard Steven say, Steven may reply, "Oh, I'm sorry, that's not what I meant. I really meant to say the opposite." The technique of having members feed back in their own words what they hear often solves the problem of apparent disagreement.

Deal with wrong answers causing disagreement. Two members may disagree because one has discovered the correct answer to a question while the other is stuck on a wrong answer. When the leader perceives the dilemma, he or she should ask each person to explain how he or she arrived at the conclusion, as suggested above under the topic of dealing with wrong answers. If in their explanations the disagreement remains unsolved, follow the other steps suggested for wrong answers.

Settle persisting disagreements out of class. If the two suggestions above fail to dissolve the disagreement, the leader may need to postpone the solution of the problem until after the discussion period. The disagreement cannot deter the group from the discussion aims. The leader must eventually say, "I see that you both have strong feelings on this issue. This is a question which we cannot settle here. Perhaps we could discuss this further after our discussion period has come to a close."

The key to resolving discussion problems is anticipation and preparation. Very few discussions are problem-free; one or more of the problems discussed in this handbook are likely to appear. The discussion leader must prepare for the problems by preparing responses to them. A few prearranged questions or responses for some of the problem areas will equip the leader to smooth over a problem spot in discussion and continue toward the discussion goals.

Part Four:

Exploring the
Variations

Up to this point, group Bible discussion has been confined to a group of six to ten people with a leader guiding the learners in Bible study by means of information, explanation and application questions. Such a model is an excellent basic track for a successful group Bible discussion.

But there are many variations on the theme of group discussion. The options presented in this part of the handbook can be used in conjunction with or apart from the basic discussion track outlined in the preceding pages. Each method harmonizes with the basic goal of group discussion: to invite and encourage everyone present to participate actively rather than to observe passively. Each of the discussion variations to follow seeks to involve the learner in sharing his or her ideas with others and learning from others.

Some of these methods will work for your group, others may not. You will never know which ones will succeed until you try them. Select discussion methods which are suitable to the constituency of your group, the lesson being taught and the time you have available. Tailor each method to your group by adapting, changing or even replacing it if necessary. The ultimate criterion for a method's success is its usefulness in your Bible study group, And when you find those methods which evoke the greatest response, avoid using any of them so often that they become predictable and boring.

☐Neighbor Nudge

The neighbor nudge is an effective informal method of beginning a discussion by inviting total participation. Class members are instructed to "nudge their neighbor" (talk briefly with a person sitting next to them) on a specific question predetermined by the leader. Ideally the discussion topic is very simple so all participants will feel that they have something to say. Furthermore, the time allowed for discussion should be short enough that no pair will lapse into nervous silence having exhausted their subject.

A leader giving a neighbor nudge assignment might sound something like this: "Our Bible study today centers on God's shepherding care as described in Psalm 23. Let's begin by discussing a key word in our study—caring. When I say 'go,' please nudge your neighbor—that means talk to each other in pairs—and tell what the word caring means to you. You will have only one minute to talk; that's thirty seconds for each 'neighbor' in the pair. Go!"

The neighbor nudge discussion period may be followed by a brief large group feedback period in which volunteers are asked to summarize for the entire group the points discussed between neighbors.

The neighbor nudge can be used as an approach activity to the Bible discussion because it creates immediate and complete involvement, priming the pump for participation during the three levels of questions to follow. Also, to provide variety during the question/answer process, ask participants to neighbor nudge for one of the information, explanation or application questions you have prepared.

A neighbor nudge can also be used as a conclusion activity. A leader might say, "We have discussed God's shepherding care from Psalm 23. Before we close, turn to the person next to you and, in the next two minutes, talk

98

about an area in your life where you are receiving by faith a new awareness of God's shepherding care." The brief, closing neighbor nudge period may be concluded with a large group prayer or song.

The neighbor nudge can serve as a stepping stone from non-involvement to involvement in the group discussion. Many learners will be more willing to share with the large group after having a chance to formulate their thoughts with only one other person. And the neighbor nudge activity can be used to spark conversation in any sized group from a cluster of four to a crowd of a thousand or more.

☐ Circle Response

Another method that can benefit a discussion group is circle response. The discussion leader presents a question or statement. Each person, usually in turn, is invited to respond with an opinion or answer around the circle. No one is allowed to respond a second time until each person has been given the opportunity to contribute once.

If you suspect "hitch-hiking"—some learners repeating the opinion of a previous learner instead of giving their own idea—you may ask each person to write down his or her response first. When all members have written a response, invite everyone to read his or her response in order around the circle.

For best results, a circle response question should be used to discuss explanation or application level questions rather than information questions. Using circle response to obtain factual information will merely polarize the group

99

between those who gave the right answer and those who gave the wrong answer. Rather, circle response is best used to draw from the participants their opinions, feelings and clarifications of the facts already identified by another method.

The leader may initiate a circle response by saying, "God's care for us, like a shepherd's care for sheep, is in effect at all times. Think about one way God cares for us on a daily basis, then let's share these insights with each other. Heidi, will you start please. Then Chip, Ted and so on around the circle."

In a group of non-talkative learners, the leader may want to start the circle response discussion by answering the question first in order to "prime the pump." When everyone has had an opportunity to respond, the leader may then ask if there are any additional comments before he or she summarizes the group's response.

Generally speaking, a circle response activity should be limited to use by smaller groups because of the time involved in allowing everyone to speak. This technique is especially helpful in a group which is often monopolized by an excessive talker.

☐ Agree/Disagree

An excellent method for stimulating lively discussion is the agree/disagree statement. The leader presents a carefully selected statement for which there are no right or wrong answers. Group members are asked to think about the statement and decide silently whether they agree or disagree with the statement and why. The leader then asks for a response from each learner and encourages representatives from both sides of center to explain their positions and convictions.

It is very important to phrase agree/disagree statements so there is room for friendly disagreement. Obvious answers do not provoke discussion. An ideal statement is one which divides your group right down the middle!

Notice how the following agree/disagree statements might gather a supportive following on either side of center:

☐ The church today is less evangelical than it was twenty years ago.

☐ Jesus was more concerned with teaching than healing during His earthly ministry.

☐ Christians today are more concerned with temporal values than eternal values.

☐ A Christian who is uninvolved in social issues is a disobedient Christian.

☐ TV preachers talk about money more than they should.

There are several ways the leader can call for members' responses after everyone has decided upon his or her position. A show of hands will quickly and simply identify the two groups. Or ask those who agree with the statement to stand and defend their case, followed by the same expression by those who disagree. One of the best ways for participants to respond is to have them stand and move to sides of the room which have been designated the "agree side" and the "disagree side." As each group defends its position from their respective sides of the room, members are free to change their minds on the issue and indicate such by stepping to the other side of the room.

In order to refine the group members' response further, ask them to decide between *four* positions: strongly agree, moderately agree, moderately disagree, strongly disagree. A group may stand by each of the four walls in the room for this variation!

For example, a leader may introduce an agree/disagree exercise by saying, "In order to prepare us for a discussion of Psalm 23, think about the following statement: 'A Christian never ceases to be under God's care, even when he is disobedient.' Do you agree or disagree with that statement. If you strongly agree, go stand by the east wall and face the center of the room. If you agree, but only moderately, stand by the north wall. Those who moderately disagree, take the west wall and those who strongly disagree go to the south wall. Discuss with the group at your wall why you chose that position and be prepared to defend your stance."

The written agree/disagree sheet is another effective way to stimulate discussion. Place one or more statements on a sheet and ask learners to respond by checking or circling "agree" or "disagree." After all have responded on paper, invite open discussion by means of a neighbor nudge, circle response, show of hands or "stand by the wall" methods.

In order to conserve time when calling for group responses to agree/disagree statements, ask each positional group to huddle together first to discuss their response. Then invite a representative spokesperson or two from each goup to verbalize their positions and present rebuttals.

Perhaps the best use of an agree/disagree statement is as an approach activity to generate interest in a topic to be discussed from the Bible. It is imperative that the statement used is broad enough to comfortably accommodate two opposing opinions. The effectiveness of this method is greatly diminished when the ensuing Bible study proves one position to be "right" and one to be "wrong."

Due to the nature of this method, the possibility exists for lively agree/disagree discussions to degenerate into heated debates or arguments. The leader can defuse these possibilities by announcing that the statement(s) is designed to promote thought and discussion rather than to be resolved one way or the other. An agree/disagree discussion is successful if it stimulates learners to delve into Scriptures for principles on the topic introduced.

The agree/disagree method is valuable for several reasons. It almost always sparks unquenchable interest in the topic. It challenges members to solidify and defend their positions on issues. It provides a platform for the expression of many differing yet valid views on a topic. And it prepares participants for in-depth Bible study to discover God's principles on the subject.

☐ Statement Completion

Another technique for promoting discussion is the sentence completion statement. Students are asked to respond to incomplete statements which are purposely open-ended to evoke a creative exchange of ideas on a discussion topic. For example, a phrase like, "Happiness is . . . " might be written on the chalkboard or overhead transparency. Learners are asked to verbalize ways the statement might be completed. A class-opening discussion based on this incomplete statement might serve as an approach activity leading into a Bible-based discussion of joy. An incomplete statement, or series of statements, may also be provided on paper for learners to write their responses before neighbor nudge, circle response or general group discussion.

Incomplete statements can be used at the information, explanation or application levels of discussion also. Simply rearrange one or more questions—vocally or in writing—into an incomplete statement. Thus the question, "What do these verses teach you about the nature of God?" becomes "One aspect of God's nature suggested in these verses is . . . . " And the question, "Why is it important to express inward reverence through outward behavior?" can be changed to, "Expressing inward reverence through outward behavior is important because . . . . "

The incomplete statement is especially valuable as a conclusion activity, helping learners apply personally the truths they have discussed. For example, a concluding discussion statement might be, "As the result of what I have learned today, I will . . . " or "Now that I understand what the Bible says about this issue, I will have to . . . . "

☐In-depth Bible Encounter

In-depth Bible encounter requires some study on the part of each participant before group discussion begins. The pre-discussion work can be done either prior to the Bible study session (by learners at home) or during the opening minutes of the session.

Group members are assigned a specific Bible passage and asked to paraphrase it—write it in their own words—so it could be understood by a child. The paraphrase exercise challenges learners to reduce biblical concepts to simple terms which opens the door for practical application.

Next, ask each person to write his or her response to the statement, "If I took this passage seriously and applied it to my life right now, I would need to . . . . " When the learners have finished writing, ask them to share what they have written with the members of the group. Urge them to commit themselves to following through on applying the Scripture to their lives during the coming week.

A Bible encounter might well be used in place of some or all of the explanation questions in your planned discussion. For example, after a few information questions to establish the main characters, locations or other factual data, the leader might say, "We've discussed some of the basic information in the passage. Before we talk together about the meaning of the passage, each of you paraphrase these verses in writing using words that a ten-year-old child could understand. Let's allow about five minutes for silent thinking and writing. Then we'll resume our discussion."

Here are a few other pre-discussion Bible encounter activities which could be used in place of the paraphrase activity:

☐Ask group members to circle or underline specific words or phrases in the passage which support your discussion focus. For example, "Circle any words in Psalm 23 which strengthen the parallel between shepherding and God's care, such as 'leads,' 'lie down,' and so on."

☐Have learners write a first person report in the words of one of the characters in the discussion passage. For example, "We have read about how Jesus healed the man with the withered arm to the displeasure of the Pharisees. But what was going through the healed man's mind? Write a brief paragraph which might have appeared in the healed man's diary that describe the event from his perspective and emotions."

☐Invite participants to reduce the passage to a brief, simple outline which summarizes the basic content.

☐Instruct group members to compose an "abridged edition" of the passage under discussion—a compact statement or two which summarizes several verses briefly and concisely.

Each of these Bible encounter exercises, and others you may devise, provoke learners to serious thought before they are called upon for comments. Often the time invested in pre-discussion thinking and writing pays extra dividends in the depth of the discussion which follows.

☐ Brainstorming

The purpose of brainstorming is to verbalize as many ideas as possible on a given subject or problem. Participants are encouraged to offer as many original comments as come to mind and all evaluation of ideas is withheld until the brainstorming period is over. Brainstorming generates many ideas in a short period of time and welcomes without judgment the participation of everyone.

Brainstorming is an especially helpful method during the explanation segment of discussion. Explanation questions seek to uncover the meaning of Bible passages. Often the central point of a passage will be discovered as learners freely suggest many possible meanings during a brainstorming session. For example, when discussing Jesus' healing ministry, a leader may suggest, "Let's brainstorm the next question together. In brainstorming anyone may answer as often as they wish and we save all discussion of the answers until the end. Here's our question: What are the possible reasons that Jesus instructed some of the people he healed not to tell anyone about the miracle? Give any answer that comes to mind, I'll write them on the chalkboard and we'll discuss them later."

In brainstorming, participants and leaders must resist the temptation to qualify responses by saying things like,

"I don't think that applies," "That's a dumb idea," or "Let's talk more about that idea." The first element in brainstorming is *quantity* of ideas. Even a "dumb idea" offered might spark a good idea from someone else. Ideas tend to snowball when free expression is encouraged. The quality ideas will later be extracted from the quantity of ideas submitted.

Here are some additional examples of possible brainstorming questions. Notice how each could prompt a barrage of responses to help group members discuss the meaning of a biblical topic:

☐ What are the characteristics of an ideal parent? An ideal child?

☐ What are some of the ways we can "trust in God"?

☐ What is God like?

☐ What are the characteristics of a Christian?

☐ What distinguishes Christians from non-Christians?

☐ In what ways can we witness?

☐ What objections do people have to the gospel?

☐ What is the biggest problem facing our church?

Once the group has brainstormed a list of responses to a stated question, there are several ways to direct attention to the most important ideas:

☐ Ask the group to work individually or neighbor nudge to select the most important 3-5 responses from the list.

☐ Ask individuals or pairs to rank all the ideas numerically in order of their importance, with the most important idea being number one.

☐ Work as a group to combine similar ideas into major categories, then prioritize the categories in order of importance.

☐ Buzz Groups

One way to secure additional discussion mileage from a large group is to form smaller buzz groups. Buzz groups are small clusters of learners—usually no more than five or six people—which operate within the context of the large class or Bible study group. Buzz groups give people a greater opportunity to participate, especially when the class or Bible study group is so large that some members do no more than watch while others do all the discussing.

Buzz groups are also convenient for covering a large amount of study material in smaller, more manageable sub-topics. For example, if your group is studying a lengthy chapter from the Bible, divide the chapter into smaller portions and assign each portion to a buzz group. Each smaller group can respond to the same information, explanation and application questions as they relate to their assigned Scripture portion.

Buzz groups may be assigned one Bible character from a number of characters in a Bible event. Each buzz group will discuss the event through the experience or perspective of their assigned character.

Buzz groups may be employed at any of the three levels of questions—information, explanation and application. Some questions in the discussion may be presented to the large group while others are reserved for buzz groups. It is always profitable, however, for each buzz group to share the main points of their discussion with the large group. Even when buzz groups are discussing the same questions, their answers or applications may be different and as such are worthy of sharing to the benefit of the other group members.

☐ Picture Response

We've all heard the old saying, "A picture is worth a thousand words." If the saying is any reflection of truth, a picture might be one of the most valuable discussion tools available. And a picture response activity will often validate that assumption.

Select a provocative picture which relates to the discussion focus you have chosen. A picture of a skid row derelict might be appropriate for a discussion of poverty and ministry to the poor. Pictures of violence illustrate the need for Christ's love. Pictorial ads for luxury items could spark a discussion on the pitfalls of wealth.

The picture can be a photograph from a newspaper or magazine, poster, painting, or drawing. It should be large enough for the group to see all at once or portable enough that it could be passed around the group for individual inspection.

After class members have examined the picture, ask them to respond in a way which supports your discussion plan. For example, in a discussion of God's shepherding care from Psalm 23, suppose you selected a photograph of a person expressing deep grief and anguish. Here are several questions which might be used to evoke a response from your group:

☐ What does this person need?

☐ What feelings are being expressed in this person's facial expression?

☐ What words from Psalm 23 relate to this picture?

☐ What words from Psalm 23 does this person most need to hear?

☐ How might God's shepherding care benefit this person?

☐ How might this person's expression change at the knowledge of God's love and promise of care?

☐ What life experiences today do Christians face which might produce such a response?

☐ Who would tell us of a time when you felt like this person and how God's shepherding care helped you?

Picture response questions can be used for any or all levels of group discussion questions. Furthermore, comments can be called for by neighbor nudge, circle response, buzz groups (each group might have a different picture), or large group random response.

A variation of the picture response is the statement response. Instead of a picture, select a thought-provoking statement such as a quotation, quip, saying, or proverb. For example, a discussion on discipleship might focus on the statement by martyred missionary Jim Elliot: "He is no fool who gives what he cannot keep to gain what he cannot lose." Or a discussion on humility might spring from the teaser, "The way to up is down." The use of the statement response parallels the use of picture response except pictures are replaced by words. It is always helpful to have the statement available for learners to see on the chalkboard, overhead transparency or individual worksheets.

☐ Can of Worms

The can of worms discussion gets its name from the unpredictable and surprising comments which often arise when discussing squirmy, often controversial subjects. In this variation on the discussion method, each learner chooses a slip of paper (a "worm") from a container (coffee can, carton, hat, etc.). The learner must read what is written on the paper and make an immediate impromptu response.

Before the session, write out a number of statements, questions or situations on slips of paper. Place the slips in an empty coffee can or container of similar size. Introduce the activity by explaining the can of worms and what it contains. Be sure to allow learners the option of not participating. Then pass the can around the circle. As each learner receives the can, he or she draws a worm, reads what is written on the paper and responds to it.

The can of worms activity is a good way to encourage learners to think of practical ways of applying the truths of Scripture. For this reason, it is usually best to use the can of worms to accomplish your explanation and/or application aims during the discussion.

The following worms could be used to spark discussion on Christians and their relationship to government:

☐ The principal at your daughter's school has refused to allow her Bible study group to meet on campus. How would you respond?

☐ An abortion clinic has opened in your neighborhood. What will you do and why?

☐ Two high school students narrowly escape being hit by a car at an intersection you feel is unsafe. You think the city should install a traffic light. How would you respond?

☐ It is 1941. You are a Christian in Germany. A group of your friends is planning an assassination of Adolf Hitler. They've asked for your help. How would you respond?

During a can of worms discussion, many controversial subjects and opinions may arise. You can maintain an atmosphere of acceptance by stating that general discussion of the issues will take place after everyone has responded to his or her written situation. You may find it necessary to devote an entire discussion session to one worm in order to insure that everyone has a chance to address the topic.

The list of discussion activities presented here is not complete. In fact, the list will never be complete as long as creative discussion leaders strive to make the Bible come alive for their group members through devising new discussion techniques. For additional discussion activities and other Bible study methods, refer to *How to Do Bible Learning Activities—Adult* (Ventura, California: Gospel Light Publications, 1982).

Growing into Group Talk!

Nick glanced across the bedroom to the clock radio on the dresser. Glowing green digits forming 11:15 p.m. stared back at him in the near darkness. Nick yawned deeply and pulled the afghan around his chilled shoulders. He returned his attention to the desk top before him which was illuminated by the room's only light source, a small study lamp.

Nick's desk was strewn with his Bible and several sheets of notebook paper—many scribbled with notes and several wadded into small paper balls ready for the trash can. A few feet away Nick's wife Marcia lay sleeping. Nick was grateful that he was only minutes away from joining her in "dreamland."

Thursday night was Nick's study night and he often saw 12 midnight on the bedroom clock before he climbed into bed. Nick had been the leader of a Friday night Bible study group for almost two years. Though he often did a little planning and praying through the week on his lunch hour or at bedtime, Thursday night was Nick's big night. That's when the Bible study came together. The more Nick thought about it, the more he agreed that, apart from prayer, his diligent Thursday night preparations had a greater impact upon the success of the Bible study than any other element.

Tonight had been a sample of what Thursday nights looked like at Nick's house. After helping Marcia clean up the kitchen and playfully wrestling their two children into bed, Nick adjourned to the bedroom while Marcia relaxed in the living room with a cross-stitch project.

Once settled at his desk (he had learned *not* to lay on the bed to study!), Nick reread Friday's Bible study passage. Earlier in the week Nick sensed the Holy Spirit directing him to a specific theme from the passage on which to focus the Bible discussion. With this theme in mind Nick jotted two or three information questions on his tablet. After some thought, he scratched out one question, rearranged a second one and wrote another to take the place of the discarded question. The process of rereading the passage and writing three acceptable questions had taken nearly an hour, but Nick was pleased with the results.

After a stroll to the kitchen to refill his coffee cup, Nick sat down to frame a few explanation questions. A couple of questions had come to mind earlier in the week and he had been writing them and rewriting them in his mind for three days. Under the lamp's steady glare it took Nick another twenty minutes to phrase them properly on paper. He sat back in his chair with a sigh of momentary accomplishment as he read aloud the six questions on his tablet. He made a couple of minor changes, then took the questions into Marcia and read them for her evaluation. She complimented Nick on his work and offered one constructive suggestion which Nick enthusiastically adopted.

Nick returned to his desk to write the all-important application questions. As he sipped at his coffee cup, Nick's mind drifted into the past and he thought about his first months as leader of the Bible study group. He had been a participant in another study group for three years—enjoying the fellowship, drinking in the lively discussion and growing in his personal life by giant steps. But the group had grown too large and a sister group was formed. Nick was surprised and pleased when the assistant pastor asked him to consider leading the group. As he prayed about it, Nick was overwhelmed with two contrasting impressions: his own feeling of inadequacy for the role and the Holy Spirit's encouragement to be with him in the new responsibility. After receiving Pastor Tim's assurance of additional training, Nick accepted.

The first few months as leader had been very tense for Nick. He fumbled and bumbled through the inaugural Bible study meetings wondering why he had accepted such a difficult role. People didn't understand his questions. Their answers were superficial and sometimes "off the wall." And the discussions often wandered so far off the point that Nick never could lead them back. But Pastor Tim met with Nick each week for breakfast and fortified him with encouragement and practical tips for guiding the Bible study group into productive discussion in spite of the many "wrinkles" which seemed to appear every week. Most of all, Nick was grateful for Tim's prayers which always seemed to leave Nick uplifted and ready to face the challenge again.

Nick's reverie was interrupted by Marcia's preparations for bed. After securing the house for the night and kissing Marcia goodnight, Nick returned to his desk to finish his preparations. Nick envisioned the group that would be seated with him and Marcia at the Harmon's home on Friday night. There was Roger and Nancy, who were mature enough to lead a Bible study group themselves. Vera was a single career woman and a new Christian who struggled with the temptations of the fast-paced business world she inhabited. And there was Trevor and Ollie, quiet, nonparticipative, yet thirsting for more of God in their lives. As each face passed before Nick's eyes he thanked God for them and asked Him to use the Bible study to meet their needs and encourage their faith.

After prayerfully reflecting on his group, Nick saw the direction his application questions should take. He wrote two of them, rewrote them three times and pushed his chair back with a sigh. By 11:15 p.m., all that remained was to copy his questions and notes onto a 4″ by 6″ card to slip inside his Bible. He was confident that tomorrow night's study was going to be an enriching time of growth and fellowship for his small flock—and himself.

What does it take to build a Bible study discussion group like Nick's? And what does it take to develop the kind of discussion leader that Nick, our fictional example, represents? First, it is important to realize that successful Bible study groups and leaders are rarely overnight phenomena. Successful groups and leaders don't pop into existence, they emerge by means of a process. Therefore a key element in the building of a group and the building of a leader is *time*. If you are new to the concepts in this handbook, take a deep breath and admit that it may be many months before you feel confident in the guidelines presented in these pages. And it may be many more months before your Bible study group functions with the ease and progress exemplified in the introductory story. Like any other living organism, a discussion group must have time to grow.

In the meantime, there are some things that you can do to encourage the development of your group as Bible students and yourself as an effective leader. First, determine to maintain your commitment to be what God wants you to be for your group. One of the most persistent temptations you will face over the long haul of personal and group development is the temptation to give up. Your skills will not develop as quickly as you had hoped. The group will not progress as you had planned. You will become impatient and entertain "retirement."

What would you think of a farmer who invested money in land, equipment and seed only to quit farming because his corn wouldn't grow in 30 days? That's ridiculous! Everybody knows that, even after planting, watering, cultivating and weeding, a farmer must wait patiently while the seeds "do their thing" over an unalterable period of time. Paul applied the same agricultural principle when discussing commitment and persistence in ministry: "Let us not become weary in doing good, for at the proper time we will reap a harvest if we do not give up" (Gal. 6:9). If God has called you to lead a Bible study group, He probably has a long-term period in mind. Keep your commitment fresh as you persist for personal and group growth.

Second, determine to develop your skills over the months and years of your leadership position. Using the farming illustration again, a farmer does not plant seed and then take a vacation until the produce is mature. Rather, he waters, cultivates, weeds, sprays and thins to insure the best possible crop. Similarly, a discussion leader should continually hone his or her skills even while the group is immature or unlearned in the dynamics of group Bible discussion.

Practice writing information, explanation and application questions. Practice framing transition statements between the levels of questions. Practice specific problem-solving statements you would use when the group talks too much, talks too little, gives irrelevant or wrong answers, or strays off the point. Practice affirmative statements which will help your group members feel at ease about attending and participating in the Bible study. Invite your spouse or another good friend to help you by critiquing your questions and style.

Third, cultivate a relationship with your Bible study group members beyond the discussion circle. The more comfortable they feel around you and each other, the more ready they will be to participate in the group discussion process. Invite one or two couples to your home for dinner. Schedule to take each group member out to breakfast or lunch over a period of weeks or months. Host a class party two or three times a year where the emphasis is on fun and fellowship rather than in-depth Bible study. These additional hours of investment will result in a warmth of relationship which will greatly enhance the Bible study discussion group.

Fourth, saturate your leadership ministry and your group members with prayer. It may sound oversimplified, but there is no substitute for persistent, faith-filled prayer. Pray for each member of the Bible study group by name often through the week. Pray for them as you frame each question or activity. Ask God to prepare them to participate and learn.

Pray for yourself and your development as a Bible study leader. Pray about the discussion focus and aims for each discussion. Pray about the information, explanation and application questions. Pray about the approach and conclusion activities. Pray about the facilities where the discussion will be held. Submit every person, idea and thing to the authority of Christ's lordship (see 2 Cor. 10:4,5).

We close by reiterating for good measure a statement already mentioned twice before in this handbook: Discussion leaders are made, not born. Rest assured that if God has called you to the ministry of leading a Bible discussion group, He will also equip you for it. God does not look primarily for *ability,* He looks for *availability.* You have made yourself *available* to serve Him as a discussion leader, He will make you *able* as you avail yourself of His power and presence (see 2 Cor. 3:5,6).

ADULT BIBLE STUDY RESOURCES
NEW COURSES!

▷ All-in-one format! ◁

The coursebooks for each of these 13-week courses contain teacher's materials and reproducible in-class discovery pages. Order one course-book for each teacher, and one paperback commentary for each teacher and student.

SOULSEARCH Bob Ricker with Ron Pitkin. Hope for 21st century living from Ecclesiastes.

    _____Teacher's Coursebook   AB635 $13.50

    _____Paperback Commentary   S393118 $ 4.25

GOD WITH US D. A. Carson. The life of Christ as recorded by Matthew

    _____Teacher's Coursebook   AB625 $13.50

    _____Paperback Commentary   S392106 $ 4.25

CONFRONTED BY LOVE Dan Baumann. Paul's second letter to the Cor-inthians.

    _____Teacher's Coursebook   AB615 $13.50

    _____Paperback Commentary   S391101 $ 4.25

THE FINAL FRONTIER A 13-week course exploring the biblical mandate for world missions.

    _____Teacher's Coursebook   AB545 $13.50

Buy these at your local bookstore or use this handy coupon for ordering:

Regal Books, P.O. Box 3875, Ventura, CA 93006
Please send me the booklet(s) I have checked above. I am enclosing $ _____ . (Orders under $20.00, add $2.00 shipping and handling, over $20.00 add 10%. All California orders must include 6% sales tax.) Send a check or money order—no cash or C.O.D. please.

Please charge my
☐ Visa   Card # _____
☐ MasterCard Exp. Date _____

Name: _____

Address: _____

City: _____ State/Zip: _____
Please allow 2-4 weeks delivery. U.S. prices shown. Prices subject to change without notice.